Winter

Copyright © 1981, Raintree Publishers Inc.

Library of Congress Number: 80-25115

3 4 5 6 7 8 9 89 88 87 86 85

Printed in the United States of America.

Library of Congress Cataloging in Publication Data

Allington, Richard L.
  Winter.

  (Beginning to learn about)
  SUMMARY: Simple text and illustrations introduce
the colors, shapes, sounds, clothes, activities and
other things associated with the winter season.
  1. Winter — Juvenile literature. [1. Winter.
2. Seasons] I. Krull, Kathleen, joint author.
II. Wallner, John C. III. Title. IV. Series.
QB631.A393   500   80-25115

Richard L. Allington is Associate Professor, Department of Reading,
State University of New York at Albany.
Kathleen Krull is the author of twenty-five books for children.

BEGINNING TO LEARN ABOUT

WINTER

BY RICHARD L. ALLINGTON, PH.D., • AND KATHLEEN KRULL
ILLUSTRATED BY JOHN C. WALLNER

Raintree Childrens Books • Milwaukee • Toronto • Melbourne • London

There are four seasons in a year.

spring

summer

autumn

winter

Each season lasts about three months.
Winter is the coldest season.

Winter comes after autumn.
Spring comes after winter.
Which picture shows winter?

I see things that tell me winter is coming.
Birds fly away. It gets darker earlier.
There is frost on windows.

What signs tell *you* that winter is coming?

Winter brings many new things to see: snow, slush, ice, icicles.

What things do *you* see during winter?

Where I live, it never snows. Winter is
cold and rainy.

MERRY
CHRISTMAS

What weather do *you* have in winter?

I wear special clothes in winter — a snowsuit, boots, mittens, a hat and scarf.

What special clothes do you wear in winter? Why?

I see many shapes in winter. Snowballs
are round. Snowflakes are hexagons —
they have six sides.

What shapes do you see during winter?

Winter brings special feelings. I feel cozy
when I'm indoors. I feel sorry for the
hungry wild animals and birds.

What special feelings do you have in winter?

I do special things in winter.
I like to ice-skate.

What special things do you
like to do in winter?

Where I live, rabbits sometimes sleep in
snowdrifts. Beavers stay inside the houses
they build.

What do other animals do when winter comes? Why?

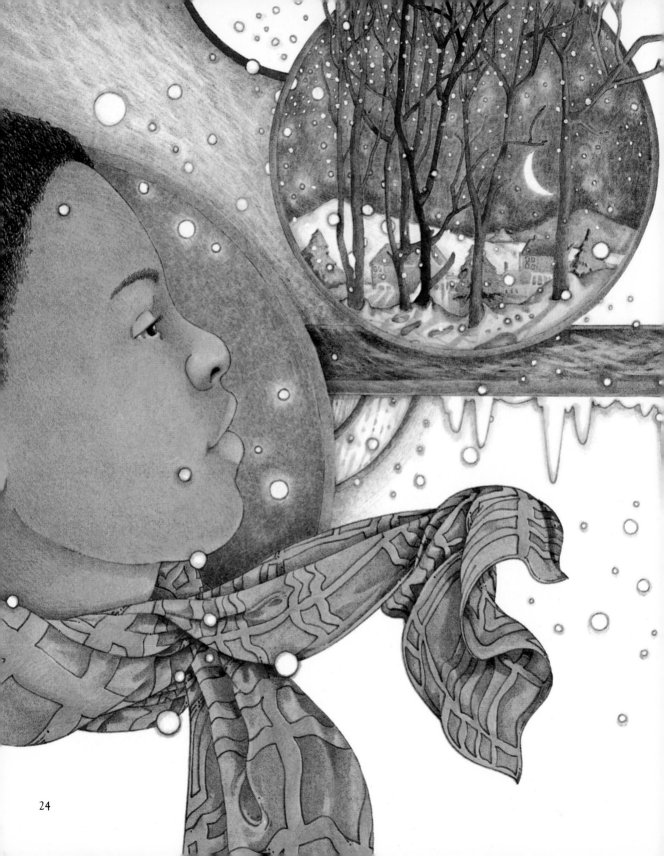

24

I hear special sounds in winter. The wind whistles. The ice cracks. Snow falls very quietly.

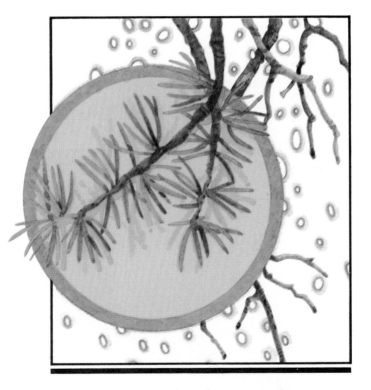

What sounds do you hear during winter?

Ice hockey is a winter sport.

What other winter sports can
you think of?

Sometimes I don't like
winter. I wish I could play
outside more. When it's
time to shovel, I wish I
didn't have to be outside.

Are there things you don't
like about winter?

I see things that tell me winter is ending.
The snow melts away. The days are a little
warmer. I can tell that spring is coming.

What signs tell you that winter is ending?

Say the names of the twelve months in the year.
Which months are the winter months?

January

February

March

April

May

June

July

August

September

October

November

December

Make two lists. On one list, put things
that you can do only when it's winter.
On the other list, put things you *can't* do
when it's winter. What list is longer?
Which list has more of your favorite things
to do on it?